A Descriptive Analysis of Change in Eligibility Status for the USDA Forest Service Economic Recovery Program

By Krista M. Gebert and Susan L. Odell

May 2007

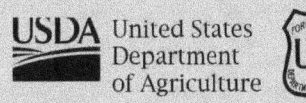 United States Department of Agriculture  Forest Service

Rocky Mountain Research Station

Research Paper RMRS-RP-62WWW

Gebert, Krista M.; Odell, Susan L. 2007. **A descriptive analysis of change in eligibility status for the USDA Forest Service Economic Recovery Program**. Res. Pap. RMRS-RP-62WWW. Fort Collins, CO: U.S. Department of Agriculture, Forest Service, Rocky Mountain Research Station. 32 p.

Abstract

This report summarizes the results of a 2004 analysis of county-level eligibility for financial and technical assistance through the USDA Forest Service Economic Recovery program and contrasts those results to the initial eligibility analysis performed in 1993. County-level eligibility was based on three criteria: (1) proximity to a National Forest or National Grassland, (2) population, and (3) economic dependency on forest resources. Holding methodology constant, there was a net loss in eligibility of 60 counties, with 413 counties remaining eligible, 237 losing eligibility, and 177 gaining eligibility. On average, dependency on wildland industries decreased regardless of wildland industry sector or eligibility status. Counties that remained eligible were initially more dependent on wildland industries than counties that lost or gained eligibility. Most of the counties gaining eligibility did so because of the change in the population criteria rather than because of changes in dependency. Counties losing eligibility were, on average, larger in population, more economically diverse, smaller in land area, and had a smaller percentage of NFS lands in 1990 than counties that maintained eligibility. They also experienced, in percentage terms, more growth in population, per capita income, and median family income over the 10-year period from 1990 to 2000.

Key words: economic recovery, wildland dependency, IMPLAN, impact analysis

The Authors

Krista M. Gebert is an economist with the Rocky Mountain Research Station at the Forestry Sciences Laboratory in Missoula, MT. She completed a B.S. degree in economics and a M.A. in economics, both from the University of Montana, Missoula.

Susan L. Odell is a national program manager on the Cooperative Forestry Staff—State & Private Forestry in Washington, DC. She has a B.S. degree in Forestry & Natural Resources, with a concentration in social science and environmental conservation, from Virginia Tech. After a career on several national forests, she has spent 15 years managing the Forest Service's community-based forestry and rural community assistance efforts.

Contents

Acknowledgments

We express our deep appreciation to the many Forest Service employees who provided data for, and assistance with, this study. In particular, we thank Steve Yaddof (Washington Office, S&PF Cooperative Forestry), Greg Alward (USDA Forest Service, Inventory & Monitoring Institute), Michael Niccolucci (USDA Forest Service, Northern Regional Office), and Michael Vasievich (USDA Forest Service, Natural Resource Information System [retired]). Special thanks to Ervin Schuster (USDA Forest Service, Rocky Mountain Research Station [retired]), for his work on this project prior to his retirement.

Research Summary_____

The National Forest-Dependent Rural Communities Economic Diversification Act of 1990 (Public Law 101-624) was passed to assist rural communities located in or near national forests and economically dependent on forest resources or likely to be economically disadvantaged by Federal or private sector natural resource or land management practices or policies. During the fall of 1992, a group of Forest Service economists, from both research and the National Forest System, developed and implemented a procedure to determine county-level eligibility for funds under the above Act. Eight-hundred seventy-four counties were found eligible. Those determinations were used in administration of the Economic Recovery program from fiscal year (FY) 1993 through FY 2004. During the fall of 2004, another set of procedures was developed and implemented to update county-level eligibility. Five-hundred ninety counties were found eligible, a 32 percent decrease relative to the FY 1993 analysis. However, appropriations for financial assistance under the Economic Recovery program were eliminated during FY 2005, and the entire program was unfunded in FY 2006; therefore, the new procedures have not yet been used for program management.

In the process of conducting the 1993 and 2004 eligibility determinations, two quite different sets of procedures were used. Unless controlled for, these differences confound any credible assessment of eligibility changes. The Original 1993 analysis relied on 1990 data provided by the USDC Bureau of Economic Analysis (BEA). Five component industries were identified as constituting the wildland industry: grazing, timber, mining, recreation and wildlife, and government. Specific industrial sectors were identified for these component industries based on the 1987 Standard Industrial Code, and a determination was made as to whether the sector was entirely or partially in the component industry. Where a sector was partially included, the technique of "excess earnings" was used to determine the part of the sector to include. BEA provided state-level multipliers from the Regional Input-output Multiplier System.

The 2004 analysis relied on 2000 economic data developed through IMPLAN, an economic impact assessment modeling system. The same five component industries were used to constitute the wildland industry; however, for the 2004 analysis, the set of specific industrial sectors for each component industry followed the template used by Forest Service economists for wildland industry analyses. The IMPLAN analysis did not include all the specific industrial sectors used in 1993 since current methodology does not consider some of the 1993 sectors to be "primary" wood processing industries. For the recreation and wildlife industry, federal wildland recreation use was estimated and converted to economic activity based on spending profiles developed from the USDA Forest Service National Visitor Use Monitoring survey for use in recreation and forest planning analyses. County- and sector-specific multipliers were developed through the IMPLAN system.

To isolate eligibility changes due to differences in procedures from those due to economic circumstances or changes in eligibility criteria, the analysis originally done in 1993 was redone using the 2004 procedures, to the greatest extent possible. Analyses of changes in program eligibility involved program eligibility calculations under three scenarios: (1) original 1993 analysis procedures (Original 1993), (2) 2004 procedures applied to 1993 eligibility requirements (Revised 1993), and (3) 2004 procedures applied to the 2004 eligibility requirements (2004). A series of descriptive and statistical analyses were aimed at distinguishing between counties that "maintained" eligibility, counties that "lost" eligibility, and counties that "gained" eligibility. To better understand the socio-economic context of eligibility changes, each county was also described according to several income-based and contextual variables such as population, economic diversity, per capita income, acres of federal land, and so forth. These variables were used to assess whether counties that lost or gained eligibility differed significantly, in terms of level or changes in these variables, from those counties that maintained eligibility.

Highlights

- The Original 1993 analysis of eligibility for Economic Recovery program funds determined 874 counties were eligible. The 2004 analysis determined that 590 counties were eligible, a 32 percent reduction.

- Using the Revised 1993 analysis, only 650 counties were found eligible, rather than 874. These 650 counties included 619 of the 874 eligible counties from the Original 1993 analysis and an additional 31 counties that weren't eligible under the Original 1993 analysis.

- The Revised 1993 analysis procedures portrayed rural counties as substantially less dependent on wildland industries than did the Original 1993 analysis procedures. There were several differences among the two procedures, including the definitions of what constituted the primary wildland-based industries and the use of a different, more accurate set of multipliers for calculating secondary income.

- Methodological issues were eliminated as an explanation of eligibility change when the Revised 1993 analysis results were used as a base to compare against 2004. With methodology held constant, the number of counties eligible for assistance dropped only 9 percent (60 counties). However, the net loss of 60 counties was the result of 237 counties losing eligibility and 177 counties gaining eligibility.

- There were marked differences in income-based variables and contextual variables between counties that remained eligible relative to those losing or gaining eligibility. There was a fairly large and statistically significant difference in the growth of total county labor income (after adjusting for inflation) for counties that lost eligibility. County labor income for counties losing eligibility grew 53 percent, versus 30 percent for counties gaining eligibility and 27 percent for counties maintaining eligibility. There were also statistically significant differences in the percentage change in population, per capita income, and median family income. Counties losing eligibility fared better than either counties maintaining or gaining eligibility.

- A detailed analysis of initial wildland dependence (percentage of total county labor income accounted for by wildland-based industries) and associated changes clearly showed that counties remaining eligible between the Revised 1993 and 2004 analyses were initially far more dependent on wildland industries (49 percent) than were counties that lost eligibility (29 percent).

- On average, dependency on wildland industries decreased between the Revised 1993 and 2004 analyses, regardless of wildland industry sector, and regardless of whether the county maintained or lost eligibility. The average decrease in wildland dependency for counties that maintained eligibility was 13 percentage points. For counties that lost eligibility, dependency fell by 16 percentage points.

- Because counties that maintained eligibility started from a higher dependency base, the decrease in wildland dependency did not affect their eligibility status. Average dependency for counties remaining eligible was 35.9 percent, as compared to 12.9 percent for counties becoming ineligible.

- For counties gaining eligibility, there was a large difference between those that gained eligibility due to the dependency criteria versus those that gained due to the population criteria. Overall, counties that gained eligibility showed a slight decline in dependency over the period (33 versus 30 percent). However, counties that gained eligibility due to the dependency criteria, on average, gained 11 percentage points. These 55 counties were concentrated heavily in the east and south, and these regions accounted for more than 87 percent of the 55 counties.

A Descriptive Analysis of Change in Eligibility Status for the USDA Forest Service Economic Recovery Program

Krista M. Gebert
Susan L. Odell

Introduction

The National Forest-Dependent Rural Communities Economic Diversification Act of 1990 (Public Law 101-624) was passed to "provide assistance to rural communities that are located in or near national forests and are economically dependent on forest resources or are likely to be economically disadvantaged by Federal or private sector natural resource or land management practices." The Act recognizes that the economies of many rural communities depend on goods and services derived from the national forests and that these communities often suffer from a lack of economic diversity. This lack of diversity can cause economic hardship when management decisions on the national forests disrupt the supply of these goods and services.

The goal of the Act is for the Forest Service, in cooperation with other governmental agencies and the private sector, to aid these communities in diversifying their economies. Assistance is coordinated at the national forest level through a community action team and plan. Programs may include upgrade of existing industries, development of new economic activity in non-forest related industries, technical assistance, and training and education directed toward meeting the community's planned goals. Grants and technical assistance are available to those rural communities meeting the eligibility requirements. Examples of funded projects include training and placing out-of-work loggers into environmental restoration jobs in northern California, Oregon, and Washington; developing and implementing an ecosystem management plan that includes commercial opportunities for utilizing small diameter, second-growth pine in Montezuma, Delores, and La Plata counties in southwestern Colorado; and establishing of the Forest Technology and Training Institute in Clallum County, Washington (Federal Grants Wire 2006).

When Congress started appropriating funds to implement the authorities of the National Forest-Dependent Rural Communities Economic Diversification Act, they named the budget line item "Economic Recovery" instead of using the longer formal name of the legislation. Therefore, the name "Economic Recovery" became the way the Forest Service referred to the funded program. During the fall of 1992, a group of Forest Service economists, from both research and the National Forest System, developed and implemented a procedure to determine county-level eligibility for funds under the above Act. Eight-hundred seventy-four counties were found eligible. These determinations were used in administration of the Economic Recovery program from FY 1993 through FY 2004. During 2004, a decision was made to update county-level eligibility since more than 10 years had passed since the original analysis. To update eligibility, an improved set of procedures was developed and implemented given that the analytical technology available in 2004 was far superior to that available for the Original 1993 analysis.

In the 2004 analysis, the number of eligible counties declined substantially, even though some counties that were not eligible in 1993 became eligible. What happened? What are the economic circumstances associated with the changes in eligibility? Were the now-ineligible counties better off, more diverse, and simply no longer as dependent on forest resources? Alternatively, perhaps the methodology we used in FY 2004 differed from that of FY 1993 and caused the drop in eligibility. Some of the eligibility changes could also be related to changes in eligibility requirements since 1990. Program managers need to understand some of the specifics behind these eligibility changes to make decisions regarding program implementation and to decide whether the current requirements of the Act are helping or hindering meeting the goals of the program.

Methods

In the process of conducting the 2004 eligibility determination, we used a quite different set of procedures than the ones used in the original 1993 analysis. Unless controlled for, these differences confound any credible assessment of eligibility changes. To isolate eligibility changes due to differences in procedures from those due to economic circumstances or changes in eligibility criteria, the analysis originally done in 1993 was redone using the 2004 procedures, to the greatest extent possible. Although the Act of 1990 defines rural communities as those that include towns, unincorporated areas, and counties, our analysis is restricted to counties (and equivalent boroughs and parishes) since the portion of the law that specifies "economic dependency" as an eligibility criteria only refers to county-level primary and secondary income.

Original 1993 Dependency Calculations

The Original 1993 analysis relied on 1990 data provided by the USDC Bureau of Economic Analysis (BEA) and applied a set of procedures developed by a group of USDA Forest Service economists. Five component industries were identified as constituting the wildland industry: grazing, timber, mining, recreation and wildlife, and government. The U.S. Office of Personnel Management provided wage and salary data for the federal wildland-based government agencies—USDA Forest Service and Soil Conservation Service, USDI Bureau of Land Management, National Park Service, Fish and Wildlife Service, Bureau of Indian Affairs, and a portion of the Army Corps of Engineers.

Specific industrial sectors were identified for the component industries based on the 1987 Standard Industrial Code, and this process was purposefully conservative. Only primary processors or users of the resource from the federal lands were included. Secondary processing was not included. For example, sawmills were included but not furniture; ranches were included, but not meat packing plants. A determination was then made as to whether the sector was entirely or partially in the component industry. Where a sector was partially included, the technique of "excess earnings" (based on the location quotient) was used to determine the amount of earnings to include. That is, only the amount of the sector's earnings that were above the amount consistent with a nationally based average was included. With the exception of the trucking sector calculation for the timber industry, the excess earnings technique was used exclusively for recreation and wildlife. Adjustments were made to the grazing sector based on grazing land information (rangeland as a percentage of total grazing land) contained in the USDA Natural Resources Conservation Service (then the Soil Conservation Service) land use inventory.

To obtain the total earnings (primary and secondary labor income) attributable to the wildland industries in the original 1993 analysis, BEA provided state-level multipliers from the Regional Input-Output Multiplier System. Earnings in each of the wildland-based industry aggregates represent the "direct effect" of these industries on county labor income and are what we term "primary income." The total effect accounts for the re-spending of these direct earnings in the local area and was calculated using the multipliers provided by BEA (total effect = direct effect * multiplier). Secondary income is that derived from indirect and induced effects associated with the re-spending of primary labor income and is the difference between the total income effect and primary income, which is also referred to as the multiplier effect.

Revised 1993 and 2004 Dependency Calculations

The 2004 analysis relied on economic information from the year 2000 developed through IMPLAN, an economic impact assessment modeling system (Minnesota IMPLAN Group 2000). The same five component industries were used to constitute the wildland industry; however, for 2004, the set of specific industrial sectors for each component industry followed the template used by Forest Service economists for wildland industry analyses. These sectors differed somewhat from those used in the Original 1993 analysis. Additionally, in some cases the methodology used to compute primary wildland income also changed.

The major changes occurred in the timber, grazing, and recreation categories. For timber, the definition of "primary" industries changed somewhat. In the Original 1993 analysis, millwork, wood pallets and skids, and miscellaneous wood products (not elsewhere classified) were included based on program management needs. These sectors were excluded in the 2004 analysis since they are generally not considered users of stumpage and are not included in the template used by Forest Service economists. The method for calculating grazing labor income also changed. The Original 1993 analysis made some adjustments based upon grazing land information, while the newer analysis used the IMPLAN sectors for ranch fed cattle; range fed cattle; and sheep, lambs, and goats, which is a broader definition than that used in the Original 1993 analysis. For the recreation and wildlife industry, federal wildland recreation use estimates were obtained from each of the agencies. These were then converted to economic activity based on spending profiles compiled from the USDA Forest Service National Visitor Use Monitoring survey developed for estimating visitation to the National Forests, in contrast to the "excess earnings" approach used in the Original 1993 analysis. The U.S. Office of Personnel Management provided wage and salary information for wildland-related government, the same process used in 1993.

Another major change involved the multipliers used to calculate secondary labor income. The 2004 procedures involved the use of county- and sector-specific multipliers developed through the IMPLAN system, rather than larger state-level (and less sector-specific) multipliers used in the Original 1993 analysis. Multipliers for a larger geographical area (for example, a state) are generally larger than those for a smaller area (for example, a county). Larger geographical areas generally have a greater capacity to respend primary (direct) income, the multiplier effect, than do smaller areas. A larger portion of the primary income received by smaller units is commonly spent in areas outside the county for goods and services, a process called "leakage." This means that the multipliers used in the Original 1993 analysis overestimated the secondary effects of wildland earnings relative to the 2004 analysis.

We conducted a Revised 1993 analysis using 2004 procedures wherever possible. IMPLAN databases and multipliers were used to assess all sectors of the wildland industry, except for recreation and wildlife. Unfortunately, there was no credible measure of federal wildland recreation use for 1990, with the exception of recreation use on National Park System (NPS) lands. Consequently, we used appropriate NPS use levels and assumed other federal recreation visitation in the Revised 1993 analysis was the same as in the 2004 analysis.

Analysis of Eligibility Change

The Act specifies several eligibility criteria for program assistance, including proximity to national forests (within 100 miles), population size, and economic dependency (greater than or equal to 15 percent total county labor income from forest resources). The population size criterion changed between the 1993 and the 2004 eligibility determinations. In 1993, the population criterion limited assistance to counties with populations at or below 22,500. By 2004, the population criterion had been amended and limited assistance to counties not part of a Metropolitan Statistical Area, as defined by the U.S. Office of Management and Budget. The economic dependency criterion refers to "total primary and secondary" income. In our analyses, primary income is that derived directly from the industrial sectors constituting the primary wildland industry and secondary income is that derived from indirect and induced effects associated with primary income (the multiplier effect).

Our analyses of changes in program eligibility involved three eligibility determinations: (1) original 1993 analysis procedures (Original 1993), (2) 2004 procedures applied to 1993 eligibility requirements (Revised 1993), and (3) 2004 procedures applied to the 2004 eligibility requirements (2004). For each determination, all counties were described according to the following: Forest Service region, distance criterion, population criterion, total county labor income, primary wildland-based labor income (grazing, timber, mining, recreation and wildlife, government), secondary wildland-based labor income, and program eligibility. To better understand the socio-economic context of the eligibility change between the Revised 1993 and 2004 analysis, each county was also described according to 12 contextual variables: (1) population, 1990; (2) percent change in population ('90 to '00); (3) economic diversity, 1990; (4) percent change in diversity ('90 to '00), (5) per capita personal income, 1990; (6) percent change in per capita personal income ('90 to '00); (7) median family personal income, 1990; (8) percent change in median family personal income ('90 to '00); (9) percent individuals in poverty, 1990; (10) percent individuals in rural areas, 1990; (11) county land area, 1990; and (12) percent county land area in national forests, 1990.

With the exception of the economic diversity index, we obtained all of the data on social and economic characteristics from the NRIS (Natural Resource Information System) Human Dimensions (HD) application developed by the USDA Forest Service. The NRIS-HD application is "a set of databases and tools designed to provide demographic, social, and economic information to Forest Service specialists who analyze and interpret social science information to support forest planning and management" (USDA Forest Service 2003). Data on economic diversity (based upon the Shannon-Weaver diversity index (Shannon and Weaver 1949)) were obtained from the USDA Forest Service's Inventory and Monitoring Institute. Values for the index range from 1 to 100 percent, with higher values representing more economic diversity.

A set of descriptive and statistical analyses were then aimed at distinguishing differences between counties that "maintained" eligibility versus counties that "lost" or "gained" eligibility. Univariate analysis of variance tests focused on differences in county characteristics, such as population, per capita personal income, and so forth. The dependent variable was the characteristic in question and the eligibility change categories (lost, gained, or maintained) and region were the factors. Statistical differences among categories were calculated using Tukey's multiple comparison procedure. Statistical significance of differences in ratio estimates (such as percent change in total county labor income) were calculated using Cochran's standard error calculations for ratio estimates (Cochran 1977) and pairwise comparisons among groups with Bonferroni adjustments to maintain Type I error rates for the set of pairwise comparisons.

Finally, a series of multinomial regression analyses were aimed at identifying income-based and contextual variables associated with the likelihood (or probability) of a change in eligibility status focusing on the changes between the Revised 1993 analysis and the 2004 analysis. The analytical technique of multinomial regression allows for a more systematic approach, aimed at modeling the likelihood of a county being in a certain eligibility category. Multinomial regression models are similar to traditional linear regression models, but have been adapted to handle discrete dependent variables. For this analysis, the dependent variable was eligibility status, with counties that maintained eligibility (the reference category) being assigned a value of one, those losing eligibility a value of two, and those gaining eligibility a value of three. Independent variables included in the models reflected income-based variables (labor income from the different sectors), contextual variables (county characteristics such as per capita income, population, and so forth), and Forest Service Regions. These variables are discussed further in the results section.

Results

Between the Original 1993 and 2004 eligibility determinations, the number of eligible counties dropped from 874 to 590 (table 1), a decrease of 32 percent. This reduction can be divided into two parts: (1) change from the Original 1993 analysis to the Revised 1993 analysis—changes due to methodology differences, and (2) change from the

Revised 1993 analysis to the 2004 analysis—changes due to criteria redefinitions or changes in economic dependency. From the Original 1993 analysis to the Revised 1993 analysis, 224 counties lost eligibility, constituting about 79 percent of the eligibility loss. These losses were due to changes in analysis procedures. Changes in criteria or economic circumstances accounted for a smaller portion of the loss, 60 counties. The following sections provide more detailed information about the eligibility changes between the Original 1993, Revised 1993, and 2004 analyses.

Table 1—Change in county eligibility for Economic Recovery funds with original and revised procedures.

	Number of counties	Eligible	Change
Original 1993	3094	874	
Revised 1993	3094	650	−224
2004	3098	590	−60
Total			−284

Part I—Eligibility Changes Due to Revised Methodology

To better understand the nature of change in eligibility between 1993 and 2004, we conducted a Revised 1993 analysis. This revised analysis was needed to account for methodological differences between the Original 1993 analysis and the 2004 analysis. Methodological differences existed for two principal reasons. First, the timeframe available for conducting the Original 1993 analysis was quite short due to the need to have a procedure to implement the act. There simply was not time to develop desired information and conduct needed analyses. Second, the analytical technology available for the 2004 analysis was far superior to that available for the Original 1993 analysis.

Under the Act of 1990, eligibility for program assistance is determined by three criteria: (1) proximity to national forests, (2) county population, and (3) economic dependency. Because proximity and population characteristics are the same regardless of methodology, all changes in program eligibility between the Original 1993 and Revised 1993 analyses are attributable to measurement of the economic dependency criterion. Calculated dependency changed because of differences in the data or methods used to quantify economic dependency.

Change in overall economic dependency—Generally, counties appeared less dependent on wildland industries under the Revised 1993 procedures than under the Original 1993 procedures. The listing below shows that average total dependency fell by 19 percentage points for counties that were found eligible in the Original 1993 analysis:

Primary income   −4.6 percent

Secondary income −14.8 percent

Total income   −19.1 percent

Eligibility status

☐ Maintained
▦ Lost
▦ Gained

Figure 1—Revised 1993 eligibility analysis versus Original 1993 analysis—counties that maintained, lost, and gained eligibility due to methodology changes.

Moreover, changes in apparent secondary income accounted for more than three-fourths of the decrease. As expected, the larger state-level multipliers used in the Original 1993 analysis overestimated the magnitude of secondary income relative to the county-level multipliers used in the Revised 1993 analysis.

Average changes in economic dependency—The net loss of 224 counties due to the methodology change was actually comprised of 255 counties that lost eligibility and 31 counties that gained eligibility (fig. 1). The reduction in the economic dependency for counties that lost eligibility was more than 1.5 times that of counties that maintained eligibility (table 2). On average, dependency for counties that lost eligibility decreased by almost 25 percentage points between the Original 1993 and Revised 1993 analyses. For all counties, the change in secondary income dominated the dependency change. However, the major difference between counties losing and maintaining eligibility was the drop in primary income, which was much larger for counties that lost eligibility than those maintaining eligibility,

Table 2—Average change in economic dependency on wildland-based labor income due to methodology change from Original 1993 to Revised 1993 analysis, by eligibility status.

Eligibility change	Primary (%)	Secondary (%)	Total (%)
Maintained	−1.7	−14.1	−15.8
Lost	−8.8	−15.8	−24.6
Gained	4.3	8.2	12.5

five times greater in fact. For the 31 counties that gained eligibility under the revised analysis, dependency on wildland-based industries increased, with dependency due to primary income increasing 4.3 percentage points along with an 8.2 percentage point increase due to secondary income.

Average change in primary dependency for individual sectors—Why the substantial drop in primary labor income dependency for counties that lost eligibility and the rise for those counties gaining eligibility? The origins of the measured loss in primary income are displayed in table 3. For counties that maintained eligibility, the loss in primary income is distributed rather evenly among the wildland industry sectors and, in all cases, is less than 1 percentage point. Methodology changes seemed to affect these counties little, if any. In the case of counties that lost eligibility under Revised 1993 procedures, declines in the grazing and recreation sectors account for more than 60 percent of the primary dependency loss (table 3 and fig. 2). The methodology changes for these sectors, as well as timber and mining to a lesser extent, worked to the disadvantage of these counties. However, in the case of counties that gained eligibility, the changes in methodology in the grazing and timber sectors worked to their advantage, with the 4.3 percentage point increase in primary income

Table 3—Average change in economic dependency on primary wildland income due to methodology change from Original 1993 to Revised 1993 analysis, by wildland industry sector and eligibility status.

Eligibility change	Grazing (%)	Timber (%)	Mining (%)	Government (%)	Recreation (%)
Maintained	−0.92	−0.01	−0.44	−0.16	−0.22
Lost	−2.32	−1.87	−1.42	−0.15	−3.07
Gained	1.86	2.62	0.01	−0.14	−0.08

dependency due almost entirely to these two sectors. Though the map in figure 3 shows a few large counties in the west gaining dependency primarily due to changes in wildland recreation income, these changes were relatively small and overwhelmed by losses in other counties. Therefore, on average, recreation income went down for counties that gained eligibility.

For the timber industry, it is relatively easy to explain the change in eligibility. The counties losing eligibility were more dependent on the sectors dropped from the analysis (millwork and so forth) than were the other counties. For recreation and grazing, where the methodology differed (rather than the sectors used) the differences are not readily explainable.

Comparison of Original 1993 and Revised 1993 dependency levels—Several points are noteworthy when looking at a full accounting of the changes in measured wildland industry dependency resulting from the Original 1993 and Revised 1993 analyses (table 4). First, for the original 874 eligible counties, the string of negative percentage changes show a consistent effect—the procedures used in the Revised 1993 analysis consistently portrayed somewhat less dependency than did the Original 1993 procedures. Second, the biggest changes were due to secondary income. Third,

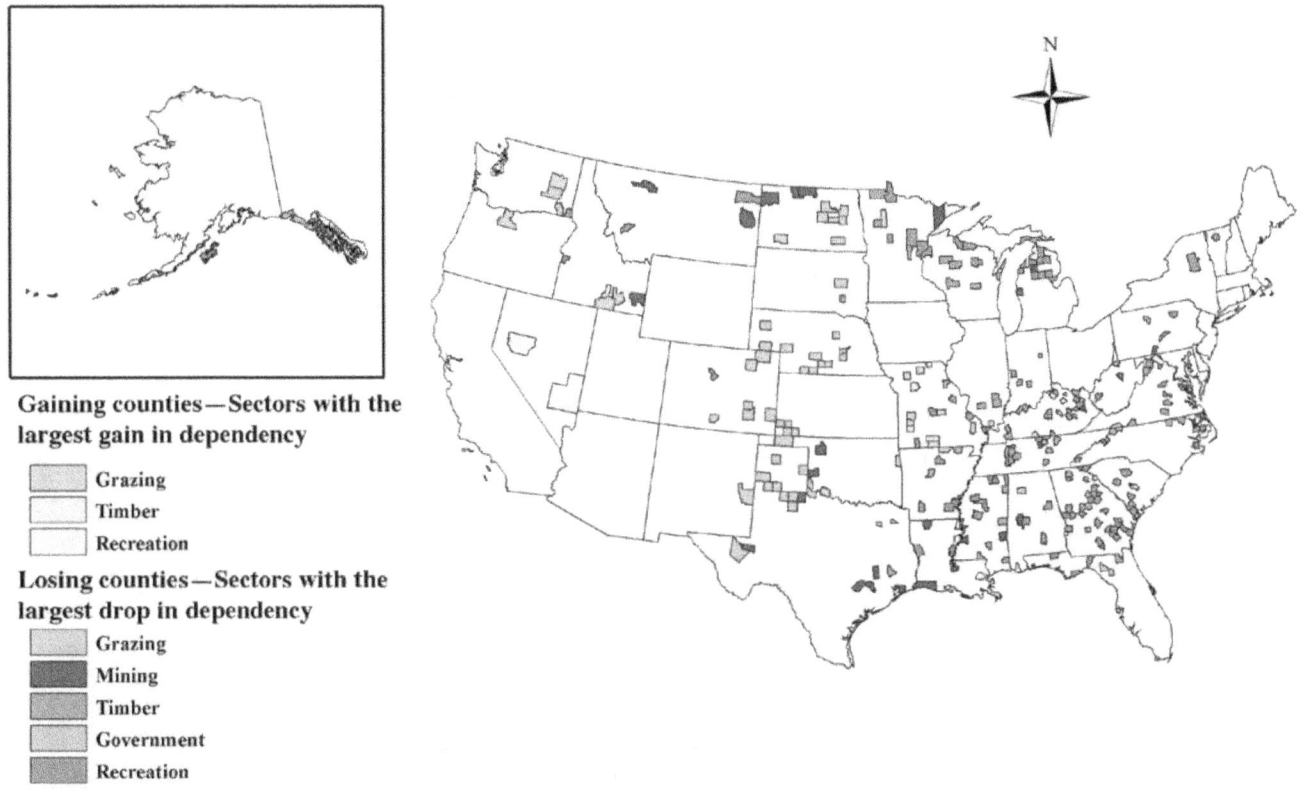

Gaining counties—Sectors with the largest gain in dependency

- Grazing
- Timber
- Recreation

Losing counties—Sectors with the largest drop in dependency

- Grazing
- Mining
- Timber
- Government
- Recreation

Figure 2—Counties losing and gaining eligibility due to Revised 1993 methodology and sectors with the biggest loss (for losing counties) or gains (for gaining counties) in dependency.

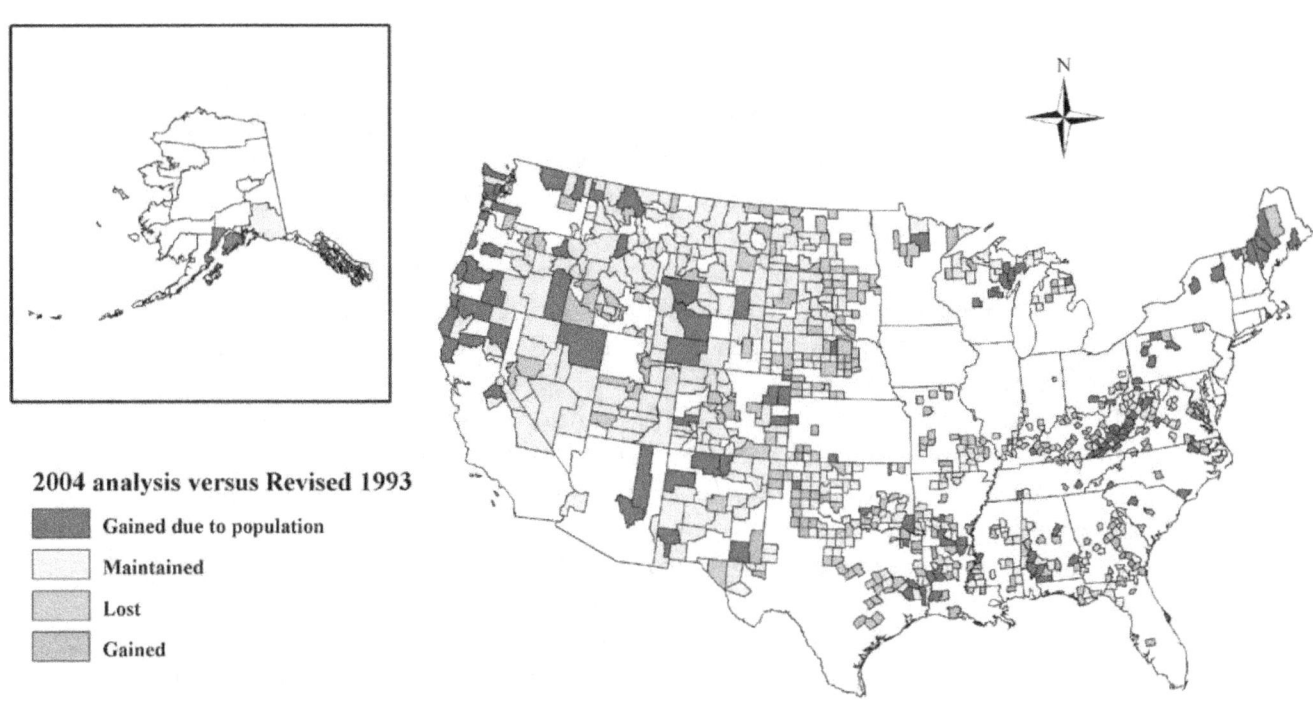

2004 analysis versus Revised 1993

- Gained due to population
- Maintained
- Lost
- Gained

Figure 3—Eligibility status –2004 versus Revised 1993.

Table 4—Economic dependency (wildland-based labor income as a percent of total county labor income), by sector and eligibility status, Original 1993 versus Revised 1993 analysis.

Eligibility status	Type of income	Original 1993 (%)	Change (%)	Revised 1993 (%)
Maintained	Primary			
	Grazing	4.1	−0.9	3.2
	Timber	7.7	−0.0	7.7
	Mining	8.1	−0.4	7.7
	Government	1.4	−0.2	1.2
	Recreation	3.9	−0.3	3.6
	Sub-total primary	25.2	−1.8	23.4
	Secondary	33.1	−14.1	19.0
	Total	58.3	−15.9	42.4
Lost	Primary			
	Grazing	3.2	−2.3	0.9
	Timber	4.6	−1.9	2.7
	Mining	2.3	−1.4	0.9
	Government	0.4	−0.2	0.2
	Recreation	3.8	−3.1	0.7
	Sub-total primary	14.3	−8.9	5.4
	Secondary	19.9	−15.7	4.2
	Total	34.2	−24.6	9.6
Gained	Primary			
	Grazing	0.8	1.9	2.7
	Timber	1.1	2.6	3.7
	Mining	0.6	0.0	0.6
	Government	0.5	−0.1	0.4
	Recreation	1.7	−0.1	1.6
	Sub-total primary	4.7	4.3	9.0
	Secondary	4.7	8.2	12.9
	Total	9.4	12.5	21.9

counties that maintained eligibility started off with a much higher dependency rate than counties that lost eligibility—58.3 relative to 34.2 percent. Fourth, the combination of lower initial wildland dependency and the differential effect of the Revised 1993 analysis procedures resulted in an average dependency rate of 9.6 percent for counties that lost eligibility, considerably below the 15 percent required dependency criterion. Conversely, counties that gained eligibility started off with an average well below the 15 percent limit (9.4 percent), but due to increases in grazing, timber, and secondary income, average dependency grew to well above the 15 percent criterion (21.9 percent).

The Revised 1993 analysis was needed to set the stage for a meaningful comparison to the 2004 results. However, in the process of comparing results of the Revised 1993 analysis to the Original 1993 analysis, several conclusions appear. First, analysis procedures are very important. The average dependency rate for counties eligible under the Original 1993 analyses decreased from 49.7 percent to 30.6 percent under the Revised 1993 procedures (not shown in table 4). Second, the state-level multipliers used in the Original 1993 analyses to assess secondary effects overestimated the magnitude of the secondary effects, and these changes in secondary effects accounted for 77 percent of the overall dependency change. Third, where procedures and information sources were similar between the Original 1993 and Revised 1993 analyses, dependency results differed modestly. This is best exemplified by the wildland government sector, where the overall average dependency rate was 1.3 percent in the Original 1993 analysis and 1.2 percent in the Revised 1993 analysis.

Part II—Eligibility Changes Holding Methodology Constant

Except for treatment of the recreation industry, procedures and data sources used in the Revised 1993 and the 2004 analyses were the same. Overall, once methodology was held constant, the net change in eligibility was only 60 counties. However, the change in eligibility was much greater than indicated by the net loss of 60 counties, as shown in table 5 and figure 3. Of the 650 counties eligible under the Revised 1993 analysis, 413 remained eligible and 237 lost eligibility. Additionally, 177 counties that were ineligible in 1993 became eligible in 2004. Though the number of counties losing eligibility and gaining eligibility was roughly similar, the reasons for the changes in eligibility were vastly different.

Table 5—Counties changing eligibility status from Revised 1993 to 2004 analysis.

	Number of counties			
	Maintained eligibility	Lost eligibility	Gained eligibility	Never eligible
Region 1	55	21	3	42
Region 2	79	50	15	201
Region 3	16	1	8	23
Region 4	37	20	2	24
Region 5	8	0	7	47
Region 6	19	4	14	38
Region 8	142	107	80	972
Region 9	52	33	45	906
Region 10	5	1	3	18
Total	413	237	177	2271

Loss of eligibility—The loss of eligibility can be attributed to failure to meet one of the eligibility criteria—proximity to national forests, population, or economic dependency. Because proximity played no differential effect, eligibility differences are due to the population and economic dependency criteria (table 6). The majority of the counties (196 out of 237) losing eligibility did so by dropping below the economic dependency criterion of 15 percent. Region 8 led with a reduction of 80 counties due to a drop in dependency. Twenty-five of these counties also failed to meet the new population criterion in addition to dropping below the dependency cutoff. Finally, 41 counties lost eligibility solely due to the new population criterion even though their dependency was above the 15 percent cutoff. In 1993, the population criterion set a maximum population of 22,500. By 2004 that criterion had changed: eligible counties could not be contained within Metropolitan Statistical Areas, as defined by the U.S. Office of Management and Budget.

Table 6—Number of counties losing eligibility from Revised 1993 to 2004 analysis, by eligibility criteria.

	Dependency only	Dependency & population	Population only	Total
Region 1	20	0	1	21
Region 2	43	3	3	49
Region 3	0	0	1	1
Region 4	11	4	5	20
Region 5	0	0	0	0
Region 6	3	0	1	4
Region 8	67	13	28	108
Region 9	26	5	2	33
Region 10	1	0	0	1
Total	171	25	41	237

Gain in eligibility—The mechanism behind the change in eligibility for the 177 counties that gained eligibility was quite different than that for the counties losing eligibility (table 7). Only 41 of the counties gained eligibility due to the economic dependency criterion alone and another 14 counties gained eligibility due to now meeting both the economic dependency and population criteria. However, the vast majority, 122 counties, gained solely due to the new population criterion (fig. 3). In both the Revised 1993 and the 2004 analyses, their dependency on wildland income was greater than 15 percent; however, they were ineligible in 1993 because their population exceeded 22,500. In the 2004 analysis, they were not contained within a MSA, so the population criterion was met, making them eligible under the new rules. In the following, we systematically investigate the various aspects of the changes in wildland dependency, distinguishing between counties that maintained eligibility, counties that lost eligibility, and counties that gained eligibility.

Changes in total county labor income and wildland-based labor income—There are marked differences between counties maintaining, losing, and gaining eligibility (table 8). For those counties losing eligibility, the percent increase in total county labor income was much larger, at 53.1 percent, than it was for counties maintaining or gaining eligibility (differences were statistically significant at the p < 0.001 level). However, the difference between the 30.7 percent increase for maintaining

Table 7—Number of counties gaining eligibility from Revised 1993 to 2004 analysis, by criteria.

	Dependency only	Dependency & population	Population only	Total
Region 1	0	0	3	3
Region 2	4	0	11	15
Region 3	0	1	7	8
Region 4	0	0	2	2
Region 5	0	0	7	7
Region 6	0	0	14	14
Region 8	29	9	42	80
Region 9	8	2	35	45
Region 10	0	2	1	3
Total	41	14	122	177

Table 8—County labor income growth, 1990 to 2000, by eligibility status.

	Percent change 1990 to 2000		
	Total county labor income (%)	Primary wildland labor income (%)	Total wildland labor income (%)
Maintained	30.7	–3.0	–4.4
Lost	53.1	–20.0	–32.8
Gained	27.3	–1.8	14.0

counties was not statistically different from the 27.2 percent increase for gaining counties (p = 0.673). In contrast, county labor income for all other counties (those never eligible) grew by around 42 percent. Unless otherwise mentioned, for the rest of this report when we talk about all counties, we will be talking only about the counties losing, gaining, or maintaining eligibility and will exclude any discussion of counties that were never eligible.

Table 8 also displays the percent change in total wildland labor income (primary and secondary) and primary wildland labor income alone. Total wildland labor income declined by an average of 32.8 percent for counties that lost eligibility, statistically different from the 4.4 percent decrease displayed by counties maintaining eligibility and the 14 percent increase by counties gaining eligibility (p < 0.001). The 20 percent decrease in primary wildland labor income for counties losing eligibility was statistically much greater than the decreases for counties maintaining or gaining eligibility (p < 0.001), which at 3.0 percent and 2.0 percent, respectively, were not statistically different from one another (p = 1.0).

In general, it appears that the rather large decrease in wildland labor income for those counties losing eligibility did not, on average, make these counties significantly worse off, since total county labor income increased more (in percentage terms) for these counties than for the other counties. This would suggest that activities in other industries increased, in aggregate, to more than make up for the loss of wildland income. It is important to remember, however, that we are talking about average or aggregate changes. That is not to say that changes in wildland labor income did not have a negative effect on the well being of specific counties. In fact, for 24 of the 237 counties that lost eligibility, the change in county labor income was negative. There is also a statistically significant positive correlation between changes in primary wildland labor income and changes in county labor income, with the correlation varying by eligibility status. For counties maintaining or losing eligibility, the correlation is around 0.50. For counties gaining eligibility, the relationship is weaker (correlation = 0.27). The lower correlation for counties gaining eligibility is most likely because most of the counties gaining eligibility did so through the population criterion change rather than because of an increase in dependency.

The maps in figures 4, 5, and 6 allow us to see the variations among counties in terms of growth in total county labor income. Although all eligibility classes saw an average increase in total county labor income, there were still many counties that experienced significantly lower than average (or even negative) growth in total county labor income. The maps shown in these figures have been configured to allow comparison with the average change for counties in that eligibility group.

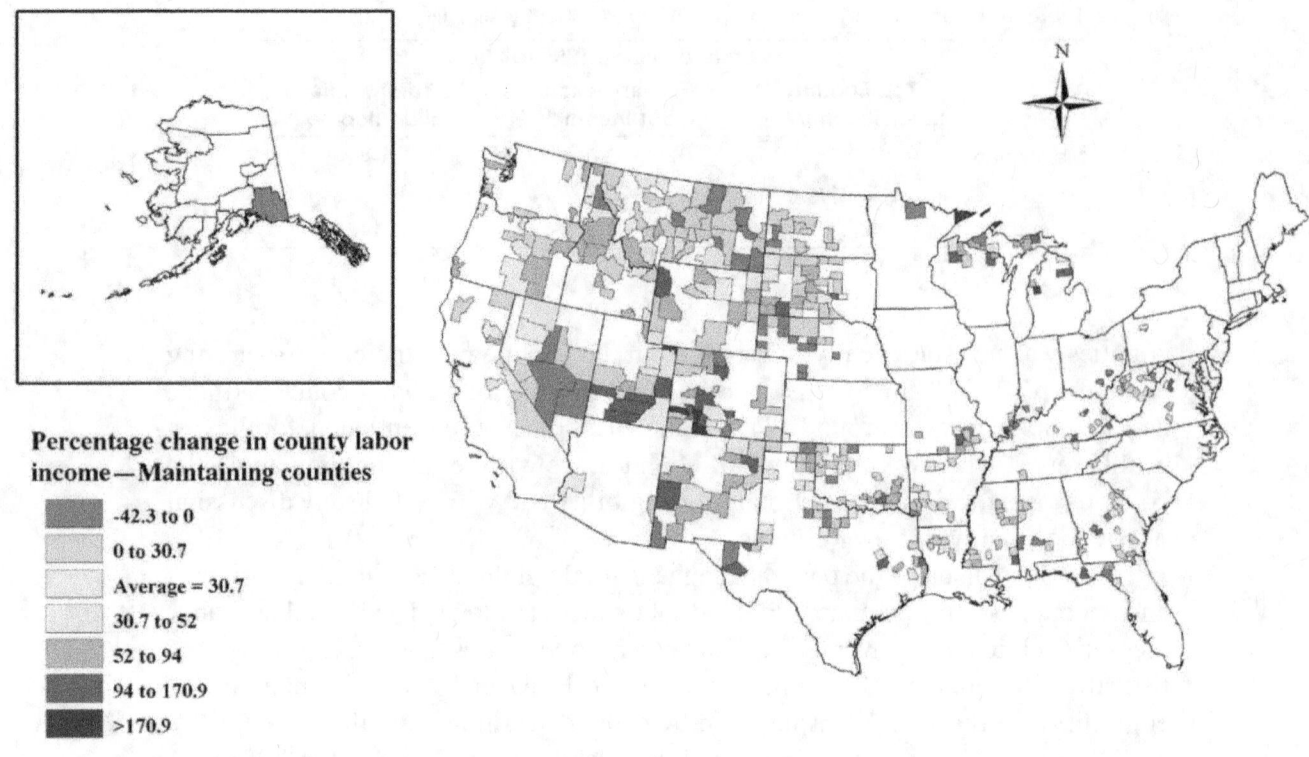

Percentage change in county labor income—Maintaining counties

- -42.3 to 0
- 0 to 30.7
- Average = 30.7
- 30.7 to 52
- 52 to 94
- 94 to 170.9
- >170.9

Figure 4—Percentage change in county labor income for counties maintaining eligibility, Revised 1993 to 2004.

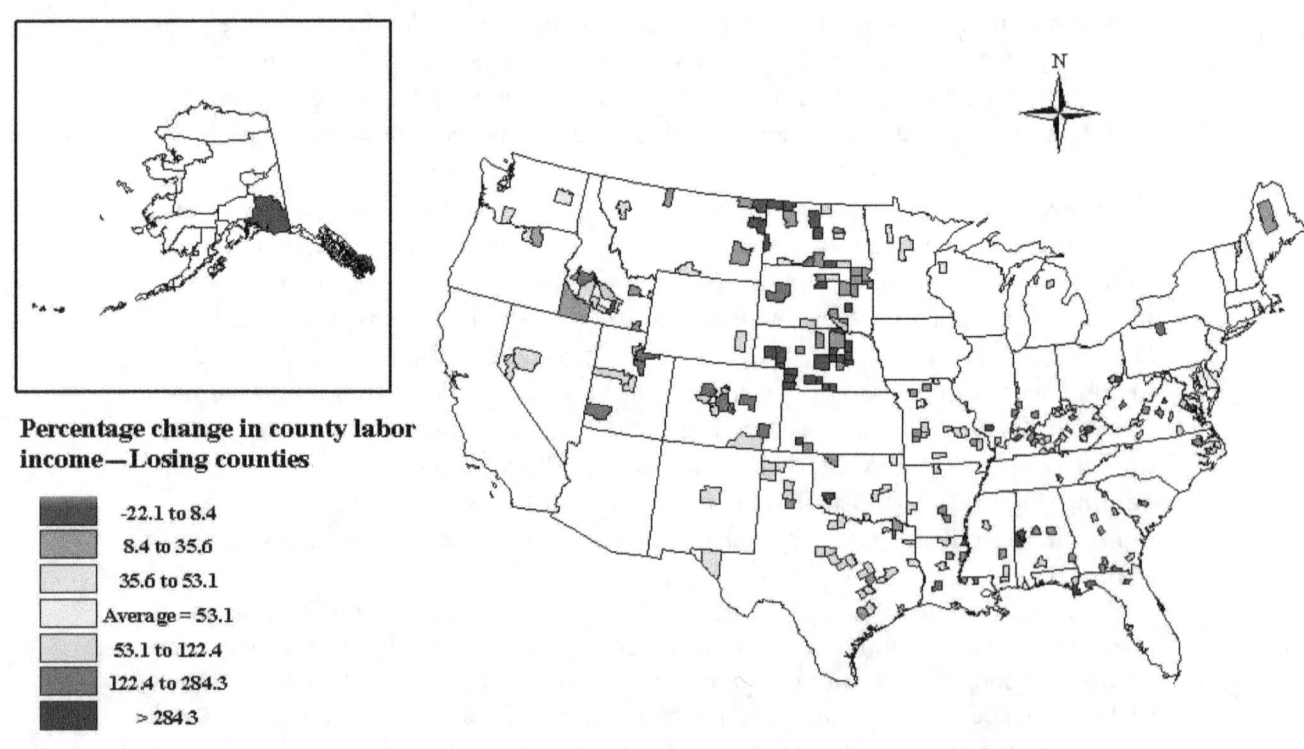

Percentage change in county labor income—Losing counties

- -22.1 to 8.4
- 8.4 to 35.6
- 35.6 to 53.1
- Average = 53.1
- 53.1 to 122.4
- 122.4 to 284.3
- > 284.3

Figure 5—Percentage change in county labor income for counties losing eligibility, Revised 1993 to 2004.

Percentage change in county labor income—Gaining counties

- -37.2 to -8.5
- -8.5 to 11.6
- 11.6 to 27.3
- Average = 27.3
- 27.3 to 44.7
- 44.7 to 56.4
- >56.4

Figure 6—Percentage change in county labor income for counties that gained eligibility, Revised 1993 to 2004.

For the 413 counties maintaining eligibility (fig. 4), 210 experienced a change in total county labor income less than the average of 30.7 percent. Many of the maintaining counties that experienced higher than average growth were concentrated in the southwestern and Rocky Mountain west regions of the country, with some concentration in the northern Great Lakes region. Turning to those counties losing eligibility (fig. 5), 146 of these counties had growth rates less than the average of 53.1 percent and 88 experienced higher than average growth. Again, many of the counties experiencing the higher growth rates were located in the southwestern part of the country. Finally, for counties gaining eligibility, 88 counties experienced growth rates that were lower than the average of 27.3 percent, and 87 counties experienced higher than average growth (fig. 6).

Descriptive analysis of differences in county characteristics—The question then arises as to the extent to which counties in the three eligibility categories differed along several important social and economic dimensions. Maps displaying selected county-level characteristics for each eligibility category are provided in Appendix A. Looking first at counties' initial 1990 characteristics (table 9), counties that maintained eligibility had the smallest population in 1990 (8,601) and were the least economically diverse (66.6 percent), while counties gaining eligibility were the most populous (32,613) and economically diverse (72.8 percent). Counties losing eligibility fell somewhere in between (all differences statistically significant at the p < 0.05 level). Counties that gained eligibility were also significantly less rural (69.9 percent rural) in 1990 than were counties maintaining (84.1 percent rural) or

Table 9—Differences in social and economic characteristics by eligibility status, Revised 1993 to 2004 analysis.

Characteristics	Eligibility status			Statistical significance[1]		
	Maintained	Lost	Gained	M/L	L/G	M/G
Population 1990	8,601	10,418	32,613	< 0.001	< 0.001	< 0.001
Change in population ('90 to '00)	7.3%	12.4%	6.3%	< 0.001	0.001	0.868
Diversity 1990	66.6%	68.0%	72.8%	0.023	< 0.001	< 0.001
Change in diversity ('90 to '00)	0.1%	−1.1%	−2.0%	0.125	0.474	< 0.001
Per capita income 1990	$9,907	$9,841	$10,120	0.975	0.376	0.477
Change in per capital income ('90 to '00)	58.6%	63.3%	56.4%	0.002	< 0.001	0.295
Median family income 1990	$24,524	$24,695	$25,469	0.972	0.328	0.102
Change in median family income ('90 to '00)	49.1%	53.8%	46.1%	< 0.001	< 0.001	0.023
Percent of families in poverty, 1990	20.2%	19.6%	19.9%	0.804	0.980	0.973
Percent of population that is rural, 1990	84.1%	85.3%	69.9%	0.847	< 0.001	< 0.001
Size of county (acres), 1990	1,167,186	614,154	1,074,779	< 0.001	0.001	0.888
Percent National Forest System land, 1990	14.0%	6.3%	8.0%	< 0.001	0.652	< 0.001

[1] Statistical significance (P-value) of difference in means assessed using Tukey's multiple comparison procedure:
M/L = maintained vs lost eligibility
L/G = lost vs gained eligibility
M/G = maintained vs gained eligibility; yellow highlighted cells indicate statistically significant differences at the P=0.05 level.

losing eligibility (85.3 percent rural) (p < 0.001). In terms of overall land area and percent National Forest System lands, counties that lost eligibility were, on average, smaller in size than counties maintaining or gaining eligibility (p < 0.001), and counties that maintained eligibility had a larger percentage of National Forest System lands than counties that lost or gained eligibility (p < 0.001).

When looking at changes in county characteristics over the 10-year period, counties losing eligibility had more growth in population (12.4 percent growth), per capita labor income (63.3 percent), and median family labor income (53.8 percent) than either counties maintaining or gaining eligibility (p < 0.001). This was true whether in terms of percentage changes (shown) or absolute changes (not shown). In terms of the change in economic diversity, the only statistically significant difference was between counties gaining or maintaining eligibility, with gaining counties losing 2 percentage points and maintaining counties experiencing a slight gain of 0.1 percentage points.

Although the loss in wildland primary labor income for counties losing eligibility clearly exceeded that of the other counties (table 8), wildland sector differences are extremely variable (table 10). Due to this extreme variability, with the exception of grazing (p < 0.001), the growth rates among the eligibility categories cannot be statistically distinguished one from the other.

Multinomial regression analysis of differences in county characteristics—To help clarify differences in the characteristics of counties that lost or gained eligibility versus those maintaining eligibility, a multinomial regression analysis was performed.

Table 10—Average growth rate in primary wildland labor income by sector and eligibility status, Revised 1993 to 2004 analysis.

Eligibility change	Average percent change				
	Grazing (%)	Timber (%)	Mining (%)	Government (%)	Recreation (%)
Maintained	−26.2	−2.8	−7.6	10.5	18.2
Lost	−32.8	−15.7	−24.1	7.3	1.3
Gained	−10.3	2.7	−5.8	1.3	−0.7

USDA Forest Service Res. Pap. RMRS-RP-62WWW. 2007

The results show the likelihood of a county losing or gaining eligibility compared to the reference group, those that maintained eligibility. We used three broad classes of independent variables: income-based variables, social/economic variables, and Forest Service regions. The income-based variables consisted of the following: eight variables representing 1990 county labor income by type (total, primary wildland, total wildland, grazing, timber, mining, government, and recreation), eight variables representing the percent changes in these various types of labor income over the ten years, and seven variables representing initial 1990 economic dependency levels (primary, total, and the five individual sectors). The twelve social/economic variables were the same as those looked at in table 9.

We conducted two stepwise multinomial regression analyses, one using all the independent variables as possible candidate variables and the other using contextual variables only. Only the results from the full regression model are shown. The contextual variables alone did a poor job of differentiating among counties (no better than just classifying everything according to the dominant category, maintaining) and provided no information that was not already evident in the assessment of county characteristics (table 9) or the full regression analysis (table 11).

Table 11—Differences in income-based and social/economic characteristics based upon the multinomial regression model comparing: (1) counties losing eligibility to those maintaining eligibility (column A), and (2) counties gaining eligibility to those maintaining eligibility (column B).

Variable name	A. Counties losing eligibility compared to maintaining	B. Counties gaining eligibility compared to maintaining
County LI, 90	Lower initial county labor income	
Gov't, 90		Higher initial wildland government income
Chg-county	Larger percent increase in total county labor income	Smaller percent increase in total county labor income
Chg-wildland	Smaller percent increase in wildland labor income	Larger percent increase in wildland labor income
Population, 90	Larger initial population	Larger initial population
Chg-population	Larger percent increase in population	
Median family income, 90	Higher initial median family income	
Chg-MFI	Larger percent change in median family income	
Pct-primary, 90		Lower initial dependency on primary wildland labor income
Pct-total, 90	Lower initial dependency on total wildland labor income	
Pct-grazing, 90	Lower initial dependency on grazing labor income	
Pct-gov't, 90		Lower initial dependency on wildland government labor income
Pct-rec, 90	Lower initial dependency on recreation labor income	Lower initial dependency on recreation labor income

With stepwise multinomial regression, variables are either entered into the model or removed from the model in a sequential fashion based on statistical criteria. We can use the results of the multinomial regression models to further analyze differences among the three eligibility classes. Table 11 shows the variables that were statistically associated with eligibility status and how those variables, or characteristics, varied depending upon eligibility status. All comparisons are to counties that maintained eligibility, since this was the reference case for the multinomial regression models.

Looking first at counties that lost eligibility compared to those that gained eligibility, we can see that counties that lost eligibility tended to have lower initial county labor income but a larger percentage increase in county labor income than did counties maintaining eligibility. Regarding wildland-based labor income, counties that lost eligibility tended to have a smaller percentage increase (or a larger decrease) in total wildland labor income (Chg wildland), and in 1990, were less dependent on total wildland labor income (Pct-total, 90), specifically in the sectors of grazing and recreation (Pct-grazing, 90; Pct-rec, 90). Turning to the contextual variables, counties that lost eligibility tended to have larger initial populations (Population, 90) and median family income (Median family income, 90), and they experienced a larger percentage increase in population (Chg-population) and median family income (Chg-MFI) than did counties that maintained eligibility. Similar results were obtained when using absolute change rather than percentage change.

Turning next to the comparison of counties that gained eligibility to those that maintained eligibility (last column of table 11), counties that gained eligibility tended to experience a smaller percentage increase in total county labor income (Chg-county) than counties maintaining eligibility. Regarding income from wildland based industries, counties that gained eligibility had more income initially from the wildland-based government sector (Gov't, 90) but had a lower initial dependency on it (Pct-gov't, 90). In other words, in absolute terms, the level of government income was high compared to counties that maintained eligibility, but compared to overall county labor income, it was a smaller percentage than for the maintaining counties. Gaining counties also showed a lower initial dependency on primary wildland labor income (Pct-primary, 90) than counties that maintained eligibility, particularly in recreation income (Pct-rec, 90), but did show a larger percentage increase (or less of a decrease) in total wildland labor income (Chg wildland) than counties maintaining eligibility. Population, 90 was the only contextual variable that was significantly related to gaining eligibility. Counties that gained eligibility tended to start out with larger populations. These results differed somewhat when changes were assessed in absolute terms (not shown), rather than in percentages. In absolute terms, gaining counties experienced a larger increase in total county labor income than maintaining counties and a smaller increase in wildland labor income (the opposite of the percentage results).

The multinomial regression model using both income-based and contextual variables did a good job of differentiating between counties that lost or gained eligibility relative to those that maintained eligibility. Using the model shown in table 11, eligibility change can be correctly predicted for 82 percent of counties: 84 percent of maintaining counties, 77 percent of losing counties, and 84 percent of gaining counties were correctly classified. If we had simply classified all counties as maintaining eligibility (the dominant case), we would have correctly classified 50 percent of the counties. The 82 percent correct classification rate for our model was a significant improvement. It should be noted, however, that the method used to assess classification accuracy uses re-substitution, which is known to overestimate how well a model would predict new observations.

Differences in dependency levels—Table 12 compares the economic dependency on wildland-based income of counties that maintained eligibility, lost eligibility, and gained eligibility between the Revised 1993 and the 2004 analyses. One striking result is that counties that maintained eligibility began the change process with an

Table 12—Economic dependency (wildland-based labor income as a percent of total county labor income), by sector and eligibility status, Revised 1993 versus 2004 analysis.

Eligibility status	Type of income	Revised 1993 (%)	Change (%)	2004 (%)
Maintained	Primary			
	Grazing	3.2	−1.4	1.8
	Timber	9.0	−2.3	6.7
	Mining	9.6	−2.8	6.8
	Government	1.5	−0.2	1.3
	Recreation	4.5	−0.4	4.1
	Sub-total Primary	27.8	−7.1	20.7
	Secondary	21.2	−6.0	15.2
	Total	49.0	−13.1	35.9
Lost	Primary			
	Grazing	3.0	−1.6	1.4
	Timber	5.1	−2.3	2.8
	Mining	3.8	−2.1	1.7
	Government	0.5	−0.1	0.4
	Recreation	1.9	−0.6	1.3
	Sub-total Primary	14.3	−6.7	7.6
	Secondary	14.7	−9.4	5.3
	Total	29.0	−16.1	12.9
Gained	Primary			
	Grazing	0.5	−0.1	0.4
	Timber	10.4	−2.0	8.4
	Mining	7.7	−2.1	5.6
	Government	0.8	−0.1	0.7
	Recreation	1.9	−0.4	1.5
	Sub-total Primary	21.3	−4.7	16.6
	Secondary	11.2	1.5	12.7
	Total	32.5	−3.2	29.3
Gained eligibility due to change in dependency	Primary			
	Grazing	0.7	−0.0	0.7
	Timber	0.1	5.9	6.0
	Mining	4.3	0.6	4.9
	Government	0.1	0.0	0.1
	Recreation	1.4	−0.8	0.6
	Sub-total Primary	6.6	5.7	12.3
	Secondary	4.8	5.7	10.5
	Total	11.4	11.4	22.8

overall wildland dependency rate of 49 percent as opposed to 29 percent for counties that lost eligibility and 32.5 percent for counties gaining eligibility. Even though counties that maintained eligibility lost, on average, almost as much dependency as counties that lost eligibility (13 percentage points compared to 16 percentage points), they still ended with an average 2004 dependency rate of almost 36 percent. Counties that lost eligibility ended with an average 2004 dependency rate of 12.9 percent, not because they lost substantially more dependency points but rather because they started at the much lower initial dependency rate of 29 percent.

Economic dependency largely resulted from dependence on the timber and mining sectors (table 12), regardless of eligibility category, with these two sectors accounting for the majority of the primary-income based dependency. For instance, for counties that maintained eligibility, in the Revised 1993 analysis, the timber and mining sectors accounted for 18.6 of the 27.8 percent dependency on primary wildland-based income. Although those sectors lost 5.1 percentage points over the period, they still had enough remaining dependency (13.5 percent) to form the base of the primary wildland industry in the 2004 analysis.

Concerning the counties that gained eligibility, the percentages shown in table 12 are somewhat confusing. These counties began with a relatively high dependency rate (32.5 percent), high enough to expect that many of these counties would have been eligible in 1993. Additionally, their average dependency on wildland industries actually declined between the Revised 1993 and 2004 analyses. Clarification comes from looking at the percentages in the "Gained eligibility due to a change in dependency" category at the bottom of table 12. Here, we've separated out the counties that gained eligibility due to a change in dependency (as opposed to those gaining due to the population criteria). Looking only at counties that gained due to dependency changes, the pattern looks much more logical. For these counties, average dependency under the Revised 1993 analysis was only 11.4 percent (lower than the 15 percent criteria). However, dependency for these counties grew, rather than declined, over the 10-year period resulting in dependency of nearly 23 percent in the 2004 analysis. Further analysis shows that 13 of these counties actually saw a drop in total county labor income although total wildland labor income increased for all but one of these counties. For that one county, the decrease in wildland labor income was less than the decrease in total county labor income, so dependency still increased. All the remaining 28 counties had large enough growth in total wildland labor income to still gain eligibility despite the growth in other non-wildland related industries. Additionally, the growth was due to a large increase in dependency on the timber industry, from 0.1 percent in the Revised 1993 analysis to 6.0 percent in the 2004 analysis.

County level information is shown in figures 7, 8, and 9. These figures show changes in total wildland dependency for each of the eligibility classes. Of the counties maintaining eligibility, even though average dependency fell by 13 percentage points, 94 showed an increase in dependency. These increases ranged from a miniscule increase (0.16 percentage points) to an increase of 85 percentage points. For an additional 114 counties, the loss in dependency was less than the average loss of 13.1 percentage points (fig. 7). Of the counties that lost eligibility, 91 had a larger than average (average loss = 16.1 percentage points) drop in dependency, while another 135 counties experienced a drop in dependency that was less than the

Change in dependency on wildland-based income — Maintaining counties

- -172.2 to -94.9
- -94.9 to -39.4
- -39.4 to -13.1
- Average = -13.1
- -13.1 to 0
- 0 - 42.6
- 42.5 - 85.5

Figure 7—Change in dependency on wildland-based industries for counties maintaining eligibility, Revised 1993 versus 2004.

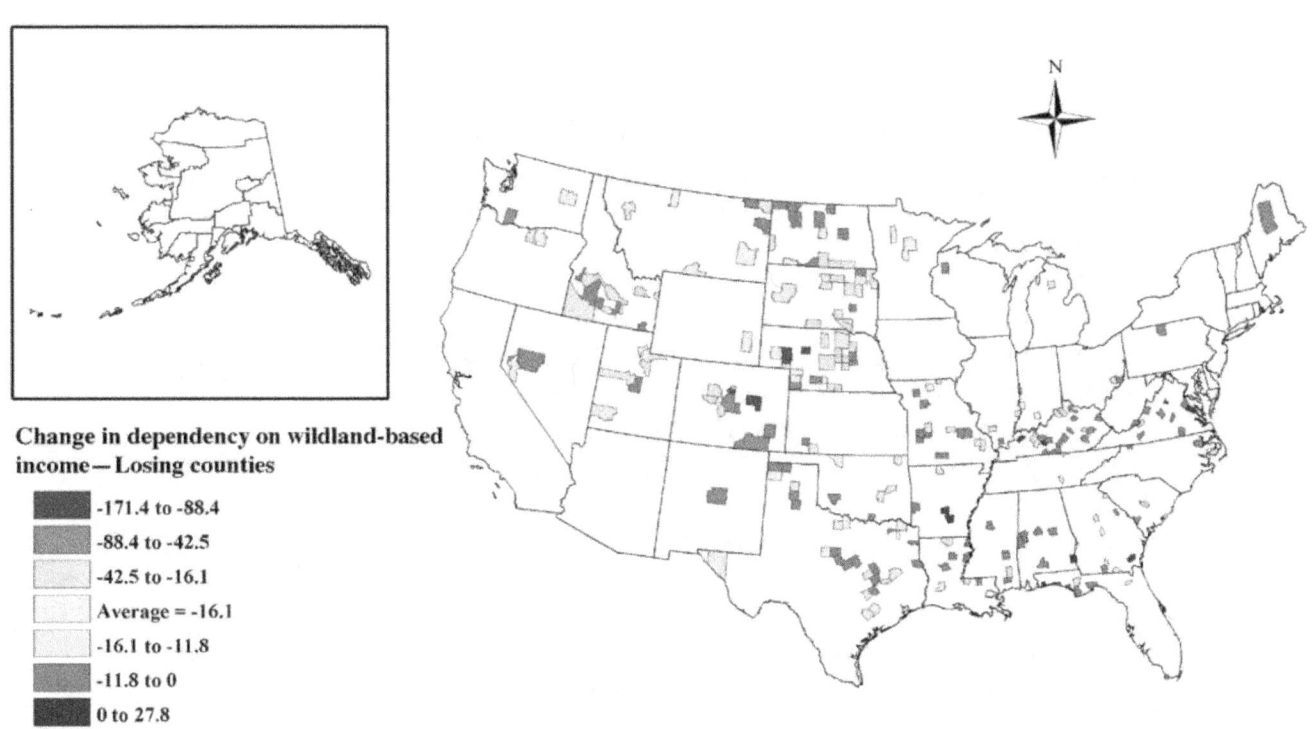

Change in dependency on wildland-based income — Losing counties

- -171.4 to -88.4
- -88.4 to -42.5
- -42.5 to -16.1
- Average = -16.1
- -16.1 to -11.8
- -11.8 to 0
- 0 to 27.8

Figure 8—Change in dependency on wildland-based industries for counties losing eligibility, Revised 1993 versus 2004.

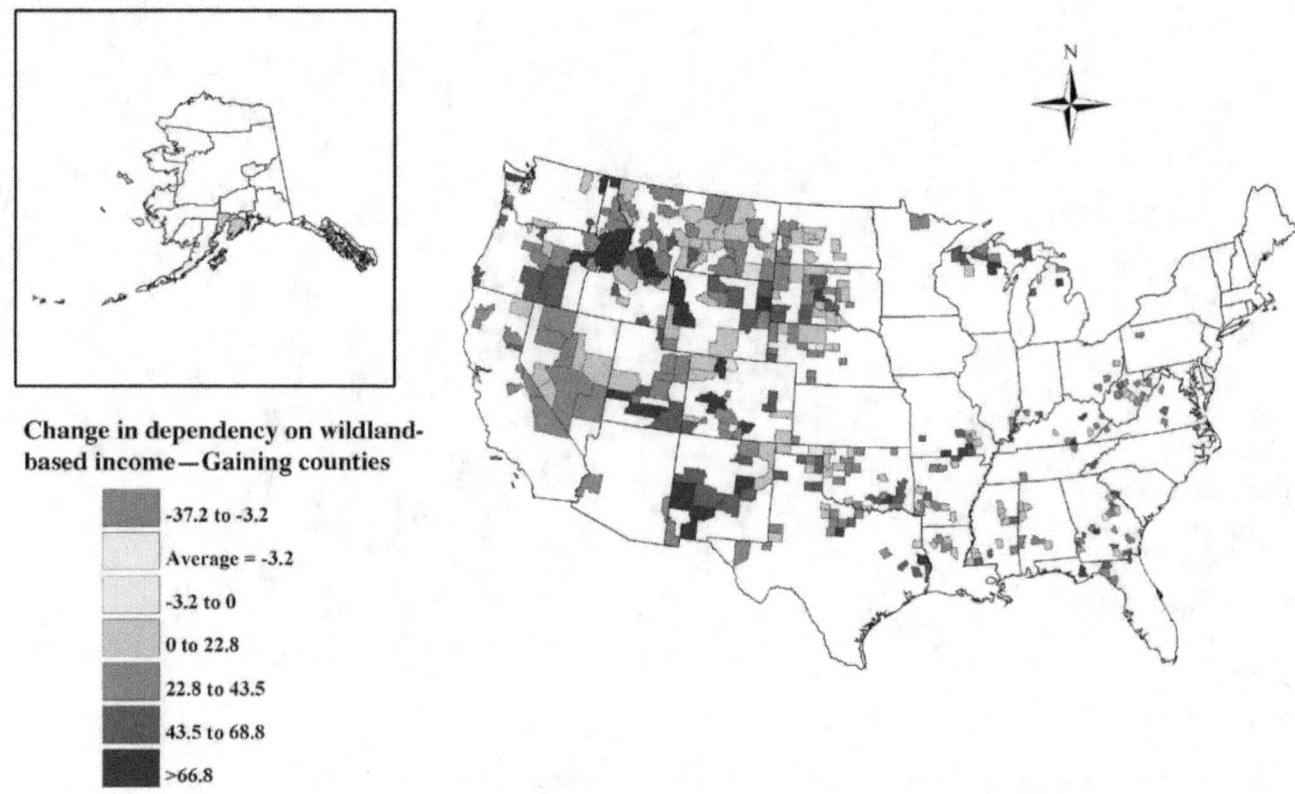

Change in dependency on wildland-based income—Gaining counties

■	-37.2 to -3.2
□	Average = -3.2
■	-3.2 to 0
■	0 to 22.8
■	22.8 to 43.5
■	43.5 to 68.8
■	>66.8

Figure 9—Change in dependency on wildland-based industries for counties gaining eligibility, Revised 1993 versus 2004 (Many of the counties with a negative change in dependency were those that gained eligibility solely due to the change in the population criteria).

average (fig. 8). There were 41 counties that lost eligibility solely due to the population criterion. Eleven of these counties actually showed an increase in dependency, ranging from 0.13 to 27.8 percentage points. For the remaining 30 counties that lost due to population, although they lost 25 percentage points on average, their initial dependency was high enough to withstand the drop.

As would be expected, most counties gaining eligibility experienced an increase in dependency (fig. 9). A few counties (those shown in red and the lightest shade of blue) actually experienced a decrease in dependency. These counties gained eligibility solely due to the population criterion; their dependency was above the 15 percent cutoff in both analyses, although it fell slightly in 2004.

Figure 10 shows which sectors experienced the largest decline (for counties losing eligibility) or the largest increase (for counties gaining eligibility) in dependency (those counties gaining due to the population criteria are not shown). For counties losing eligibility, the grazing sector experienced the largest decline in dependency in 121 counties, followed by timber (70 counties) and mining (46 counties). Of the 55 counties that gained eligibility due to increases in dependency, the mining and timber sectors had the largest increases in dependency for 27 and 24 counties, respectively. Grazing showed the largest increase for only four of the gaining counties.

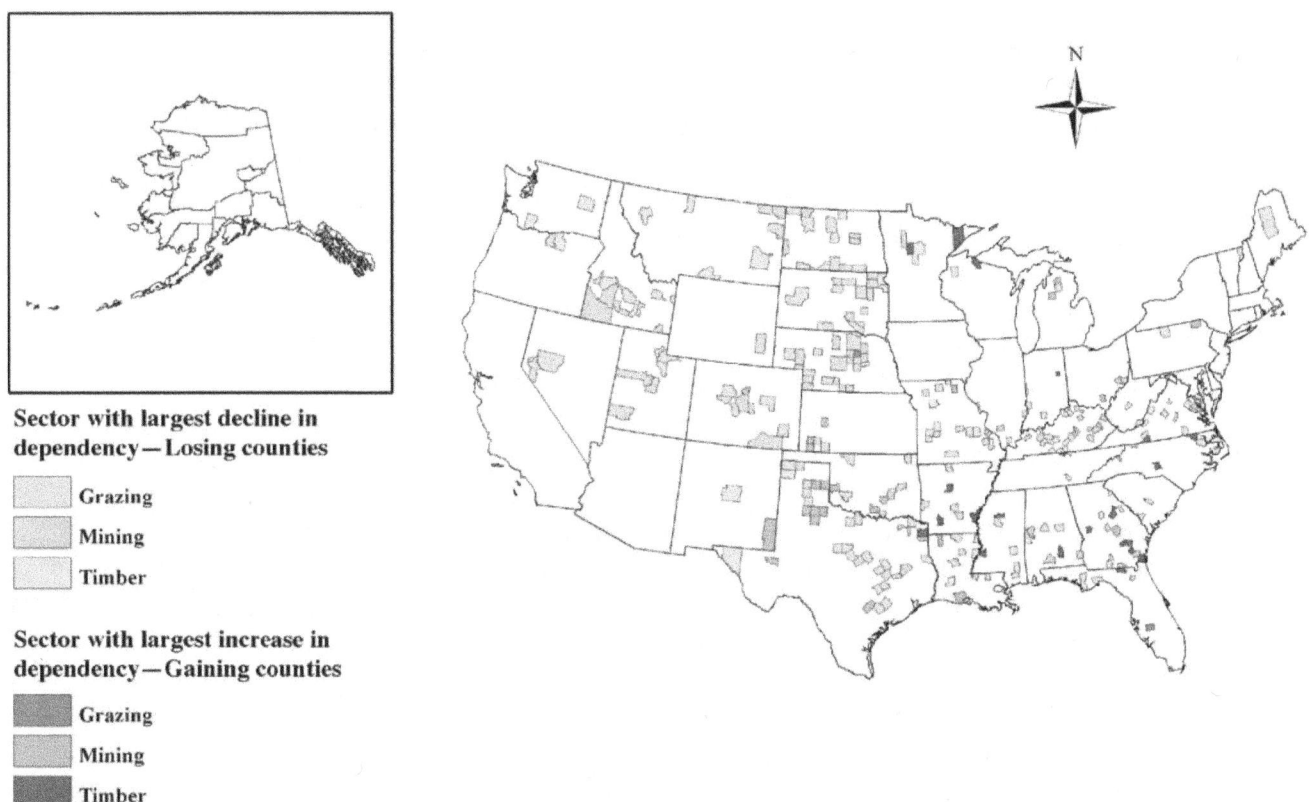

Sector with largest decline in
dependency—Losing counties

   Grazing

   Mining

   Timber

Sector with largest increase in
dependency—Gaining counties

   Grazing

   Mining

   Timber

Figure 10—Counties losing and gaining eligibility due to dependency and sectors with the biggest loss (for losing counties) or gains (for gaining counties) in dependency, Revised 1993 versus 2004.

Discussion

The purpose of this study was to assess changes in eligibility for funding under the Economic Recovery Program controlling for methodological changes that occurred in analysis between 1993 and 2004. Results showed a net loss of 284 counties. Change in methodology accounted for 244 of the counties. When the 1993 analysis was revised to reflect the new methodology, rural counties were found to be substantially less dependent on wildland industries versus the Original 1993 procedures. The main areas of difference were the estimates of secondary income and changes in how labor income was calculated in the grazing, timber, and recreation sectors. These results show that analysis procedures are very important and can have a large effect on eligibility calculations. However, we believe the methodology used in FY 2004 was superior to that used originally in 1993 and recommend this 2004 methodology be followed for subsequent updates.

When methodology was held constant, there was a net loss of 60 counties with 413 counties remaining eligible, 237 losing eligibility, and 177 gaining eligibility. A detailed analysis of initial wildland dependence and associated changes clearly showed that counties remaining eligible between the Revised 1993 and 2004 analyses were initially more dependent on wildland industries (49 percent) than were counties that lost eligibility (29 percent) or counties that gained eligibility

(32.5 percent). On average, dependency on wildland industries decreased between the Revised 1993 and 2004 analyses, regardless of wildland industry sector, and regardless of whether the county maintained or lost eligibility. However, for those counties gaining eligibility, there was a large difference between those that gained due to the dependency criteria versus those that gained due to the population criteria. Overall, counties that gained eligibility showed little change in dependency (32.5 versus 29.3 percent). However, separating out the counties that gained due to the dependency criterion, we see that those counties, on average, gained 11 percentage points, which was about evenly split between primary timber labor income and secondary labor income. These 55 counties were concentrated heavily in the east and south, with these regions accounting for more than 87 percent of the 55 counties.

In the introduction we asked the question: were now ineligible counties better off, more diverse, and simply no longer dependent on forest resources? The results of this eligibility analysis indicate that, on average, the answer is yes. Counties that lost eligibility between the Revised 1993 and 2004 analyses appear to be better off in terms of growth in total county labor income than either counties that remained eligible or counties that gained eligibility. Additionally, on average, counties that lost eligibility also saw a larger percentage increase in population, per capita income, and median family income than counties that maintained or gained eligibility, indicating that for many of the counties that lost eligibility, new or existing industries may have stepped in to fill the void left by the decrease in wildland income.

This is not to say that some individual counties did not suffer greatly because of a loss in wildland income. In fact, it seems that those counties that maintained eligibility in the 2004 analysis suffered more economically than those that fell from eligibility. Indicators of economic well being show that these counties may have suffered as a result of the large drop in wildland income, with the average change in total county labor income being lower for these counties than for the other counties.

Management Implications

The National Forest-Dependent Rural Communities Economic Diversification Act of 1990 contains some of the most explicit criteria for eligibility of any Forest Service programs authorized to assist rural communities. However, the methodologies and data available to program managers for implementing those criteria were not well developed or easily accessible at the beginning of the program, which was funded under the name "Economic Recovery." As this research indicates, methods of analysis have improved over time (in other words, IMPLAN) and new, contextual information can provide better information on factors related to economic changes in rural communities associated with forestry and natural resource-based industries.

What this study does not include is any analysis of changes occurring in the natural resource-based economy that don't fit within the sectors assessed in this study. As mentioned earlier in the report, the 2004 analysis of economic dependency eliminated some timber/wood-related industrial sectors that most economists do not consider sources of "primary" income, for example, secondary-processing millwork, pallets, and so forth. However, in small, rural, natural resource-dependent communities, such industries may be filling the economic role previously held by lumber mills or other major industries. Other research has been done to consider the change in mill capacity in the U.S., but that information was not used to look at changes in rural community dependency on timber/wood manufacturing.

This study did not have the resources to establish methodology and data comparable to IMPLAN that could include as primary income the newer niche markets and industries that are proving to be the economic engines in many rural places. High-end, custom-designed furniture, often produced from small diameter or previously unmarketable tree species, is just one example of the data missing when the "furniture sector" is not included in an analysis of economic dependency. This "niche market" industry is not going to grow into a major employer, but it has changed the way many local economies work – more on an entrepreneurial approach than industrial development. "Restoration forestry" is a new industry that isn't even categorized in the coding used by IMPLAN or other economic analysis protocols, but it does have the potential of growing as an employer of skilled labor or as a business source for contractors.

Application of the new eligibility methodology needs to consider the elements that still cannot be directly calculated with current data or analysis procedures. Also, the 15 percent dependency criterion (set by the 1990 Act) may not be the most effective measure of whether a county is in need of assistance. In fact the study found that changes in wildland labor income in those counties losing eligibility was not always due to a positive change in economics, with 24 of counties that lost eligibility experiencing a negative change in county labor income. Therefore, automatically eliminating a county from receiving assistance based on the new methodology, without looking at the whole picture, could be premature. Economic analysis can not fully replace the on-the-ground knowledge, analysis, and decision-making skills of a program manager.

Managers of the Economic Recovery program also need to look at the economic and contextual information used in the 2004 analysis to ask and answer the question: "Is economic dependency on conventional forestry and natural resource-based industries (which tend to be declining in many rural areas) an effective way to determine which communities need assistance from the Forest Service to diversify local economies and develop sustainable solutions to their economic challenges?" This study was not intended to answer that question, but it provides some significant information to consider.

Additional research would add to the benefit managers of the Economic Recovery program have received from the 2004 analysis. A closer look at factors such as county labor income, per capita and median family income, and diversity of the economic base could better inform program managers where to direct their assistance, how to allocate funds or other resources, and how best to evaluate the results of the program. Further research would also be needed to determine whether or not, in counties losing eligibility, new or existing industries filled the void left by the decrease of wildland income for those counties, and what role, if any, was played by the Economic Recovery program or other Forest Service rural community assistance efforts.

References

Cochran, William G. 1977. Sampling techniques. New York: John Wiley & Sons. p 150-157.

Federal Grants Wire, ed. 2006. National Forest-Dependent Rural Communities (10.670), [online]. Available: http://www.federalgrantswire.com/national_forestdependent_rural_communities.html [2006, June 7].

Minnesota IMPLAN Group, Inc. 2000. IMPLAN professional version 2.0: social accounting and impact analysis software. Stillwater, Minnesota: Minnesota IMPLAN Group, Inc. 418 p.

USDA Forest Service. 2003. NRIS Human Dimensions application client version 1.1. Available: http://www.fs.fed.us/emc/nris/hd/.

Appendix A

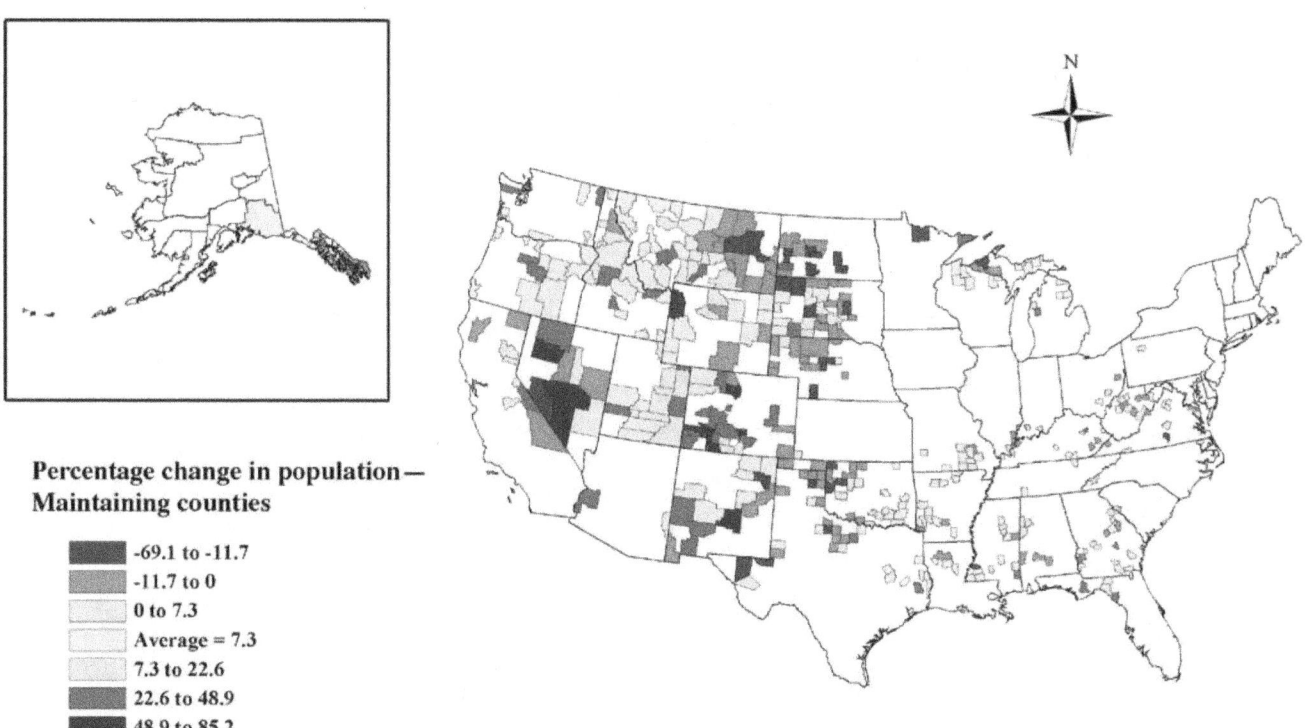

Percentage change in population— Maintaining counties

- -69.1 to -11.7
- -11.7 to 0
- 0 to 7.3
- Average = 7.3
- 7.3 to 22.6
- 22.6 to 48.9
- 48.9 to 85.2

Figure A1—Percentage change in population for counties maintaining eligibility, Revised 1993 versus 2004.

Percentage change in population—Losing counties

- -25.3 to -7.6
- -7.6 to 0
- 0 to 12.4
- Average = 12.4
- 12.4 to 29
- 29 to 55
- 55 to 106

Figure A2—Percentage change in population for counties losing eligibility, Revised 1993 versus 2004.

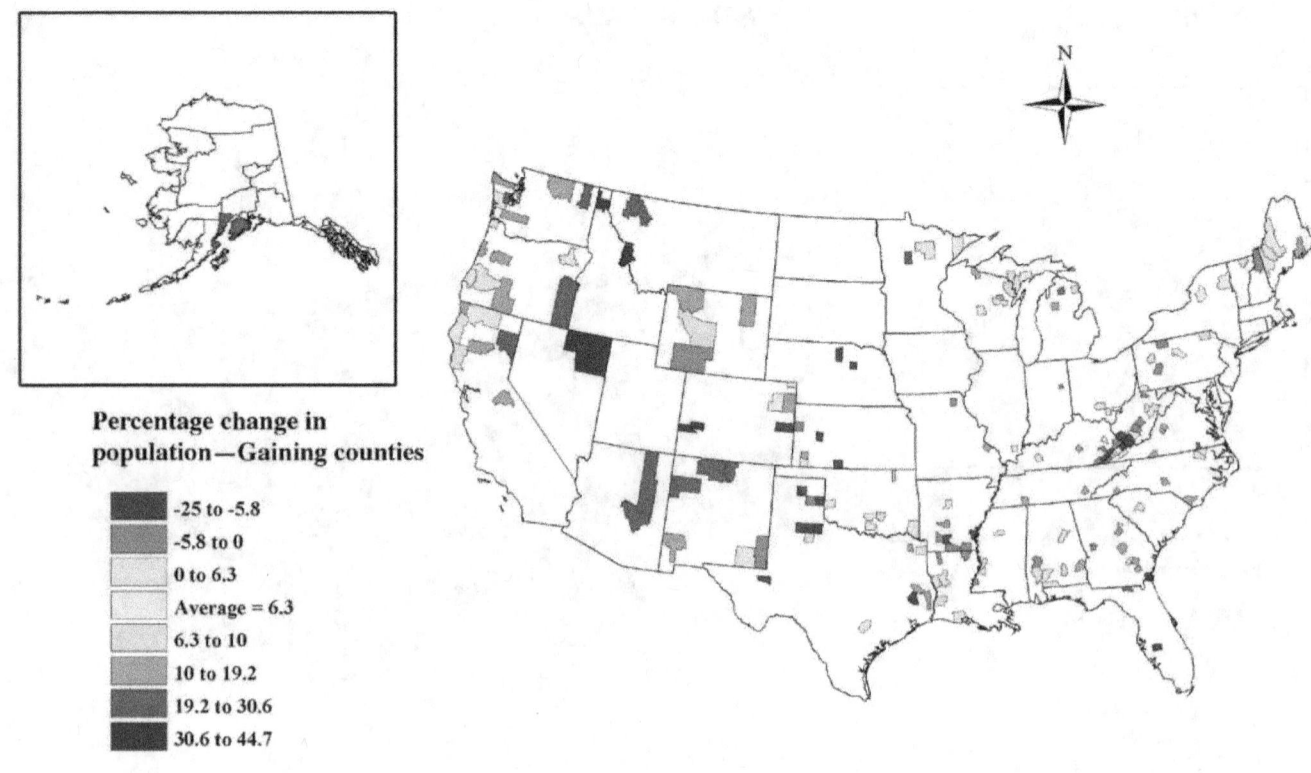

Percentage change in population—Gaining counties

- -25 to -5.8
- -5.8 to 0
- 0 to 6.3
- Average = 6.3
- 6.3 to 10
- 10 to 19.2
- 19.2 to 30.6
- 30.6 to 44.7

Figure A3—Percentage change in population for counties gaining eligibility, Revised 1993 versus 2004.

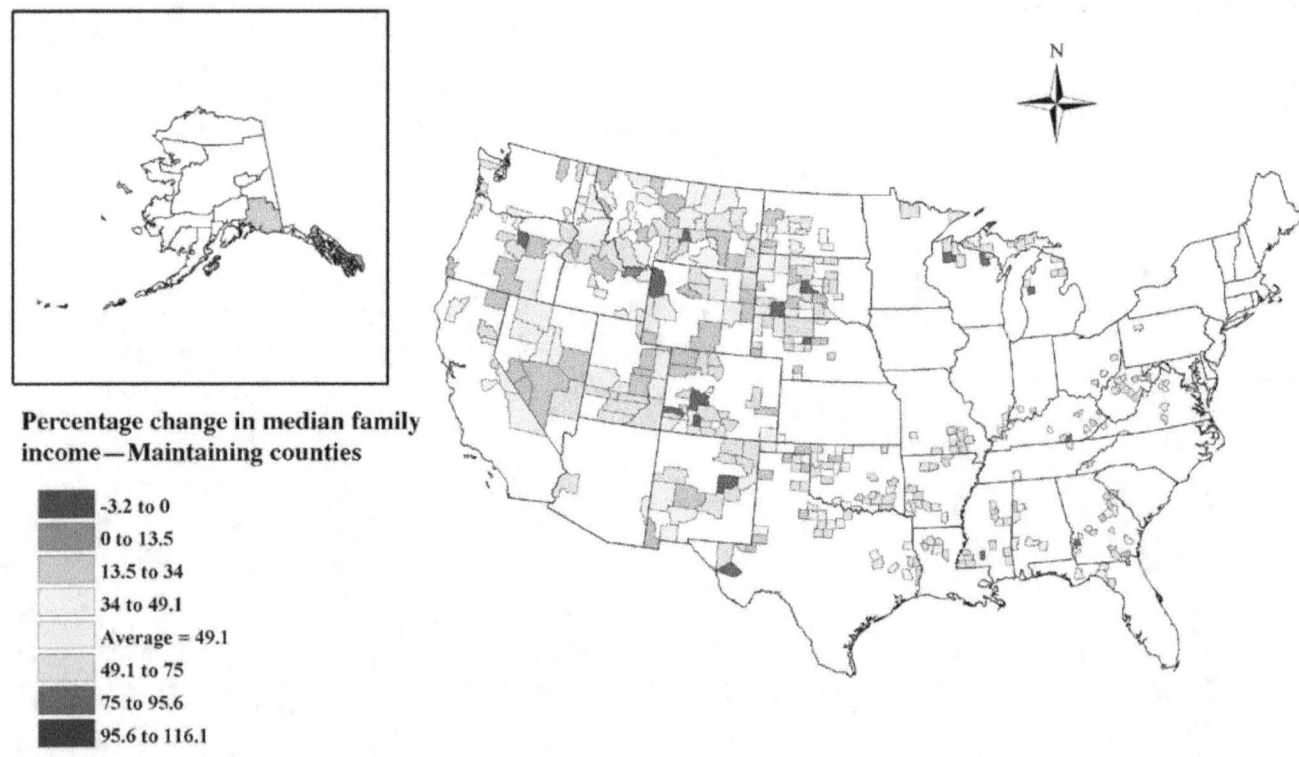

Percentage change in median family income—Maintaining counties

- -3.2 to 0
- 0 to 13.5
- 13.5 to 34
- 34 to 49.1
- Average = 49.1
- 49.1 to 75
- 75 to 95.6
- 95.6 to 116.1

Figure A4—Percentage change in median family income for counties maintaining eligibility, Revised 1993 versus 2004.

USDA Forest Service Res. Pap. RMRS-RP-62WWW. 2007

Percentage change in median family income—Losing counties

- 0 to 13.5
- 13.5 to 34
- 34 to 53.8
- Average = 53.8
- 53.8 to 75
- 75 to 95.6
- 95.6 to 116.1

Figure A5—Percentage change in median family income for counties losing eligibility, Revised 1993 versus 2004.

Percentage change in median family income—Gaining counties

- 0 to 13.5
- 13.5 to 34
- 34 to 49.1
- Average = 49.1
- 49.1 to 75
- 75 to 95.6

Figure A6—Percentage change in median family income for counties gaining eligibility, Revised 1993 versus 2004.

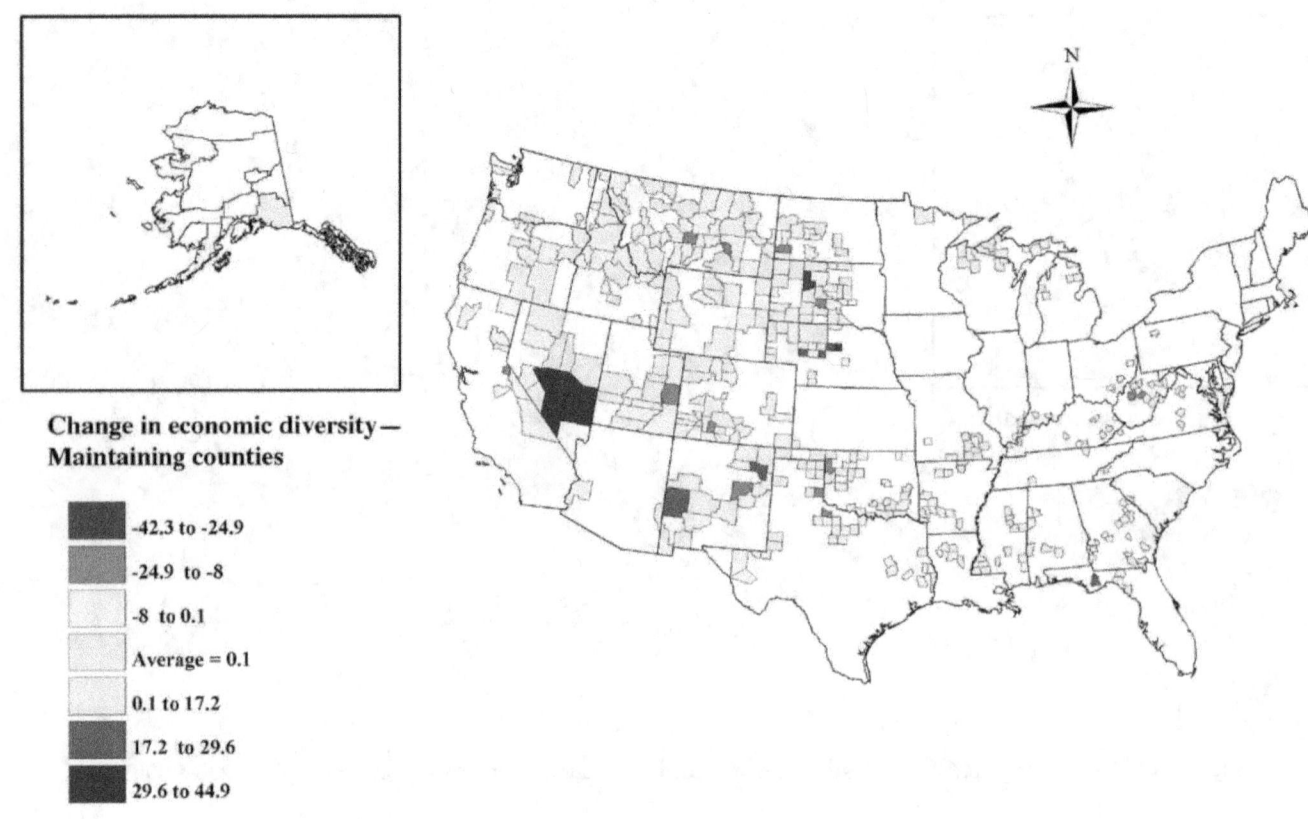

**Change in economic diversity—
Maintaining counties**

- -42.3 to -24.9
- -24.9 to -8
- -8 to 0.1
- Average = 0.1
- 0.1 to 17.2
- 17.2 to 29.6
- 29.6 to 44.9

Figure A7—Percentage change in economic diversity for counties maintaining eligibility, Revised 1993 versus 2004.

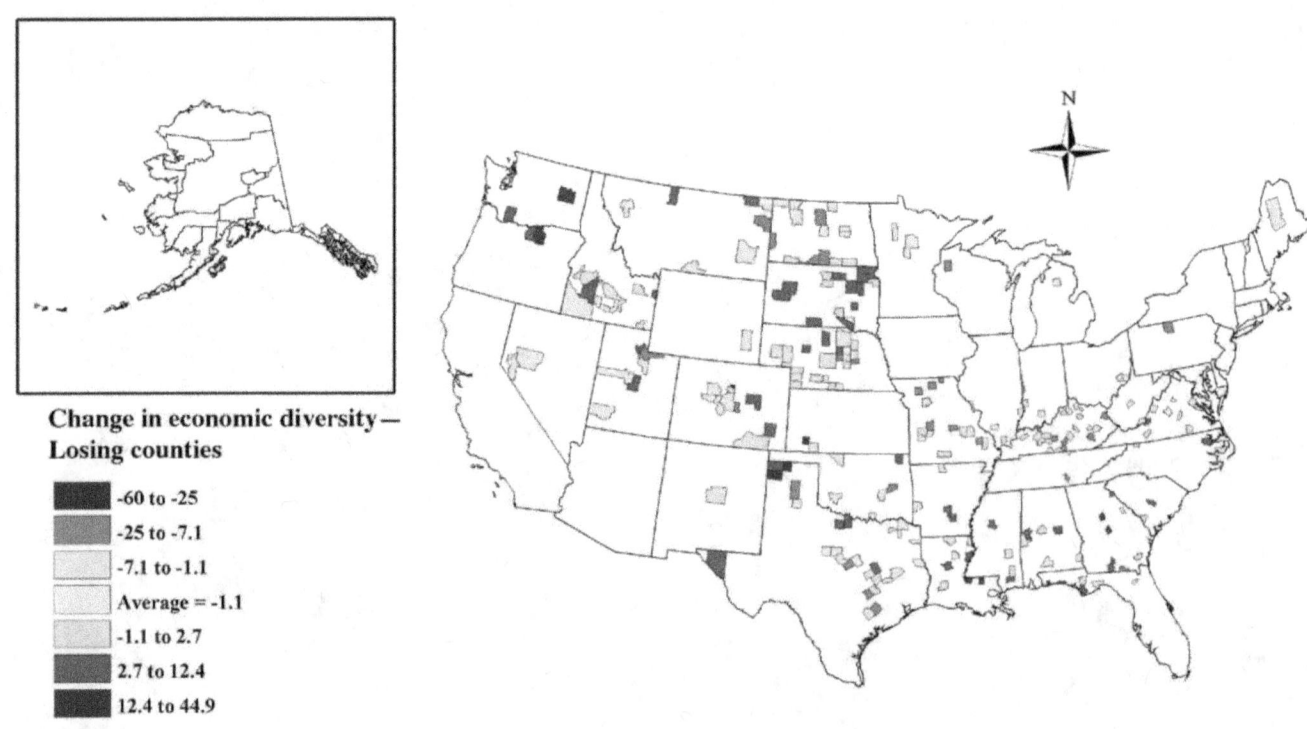

**Change in economic diversity—
Losing counties**

- -60 to -25
- -25 to -7.1
- -7.1 to -1.1
- Average = -1.1
- -1.1 to 2.7
- 2.7 to 12.4
- 12.4 to 44.9

Figure A8—Percentage change in economic diversity for counties losing eligibility, Revised 1993 versus 2004.

USDA Forest Service Res. Pap. RMRS-RP-62WWW. 2007

Change in economic diversity — Gaining counties

- -24.9 to -15
- -15 to -8
- -8 to -2
- Average = -2
- -2 to 17.2
- 17.2 to 29.6

Figure A9—Percentage change in economic diversity for counties gaining eligibility, Revised 1993 versus 2004.

Percent NFS land — Maintaining counties

- <15.6
- 15.6 to 31.2
- 31.2 to 46.8
- 46.8 to 62.4
- 62.4 to 78
- 78 to 93.6

Figure A10—Percentage of National Forest System land, counties maintaining eligibility, Revised 1993 versus 2004.

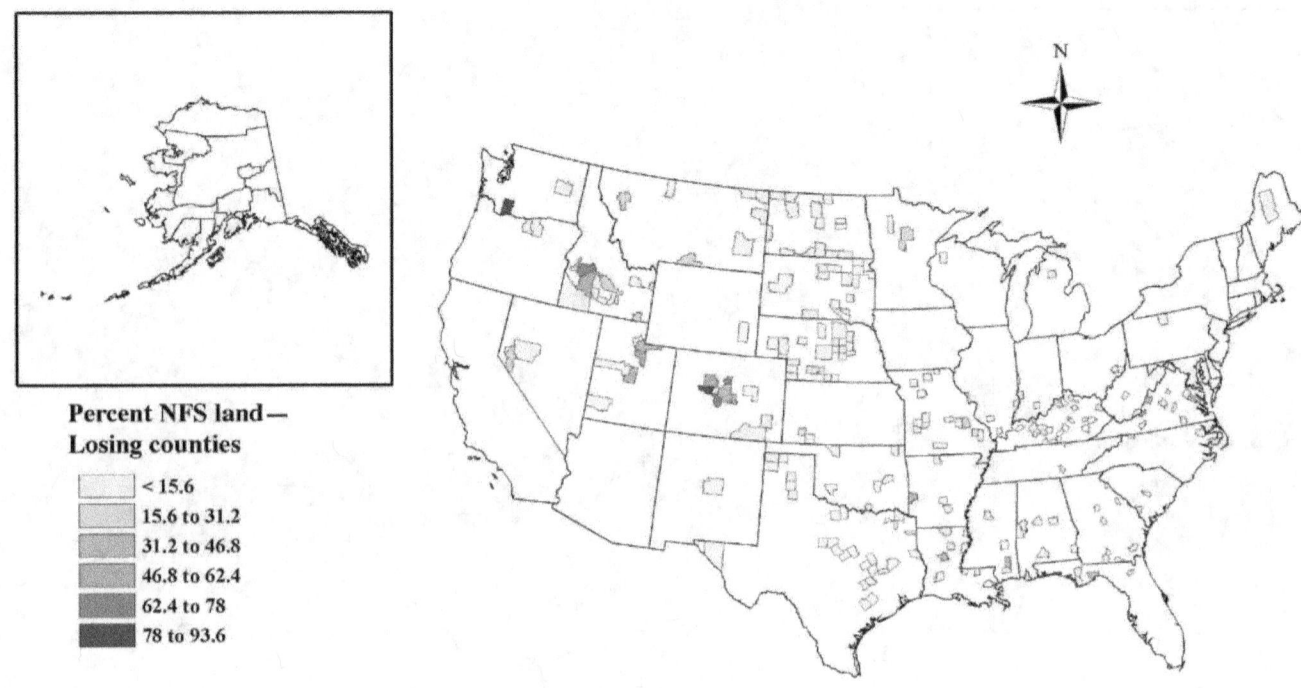

**Percent NFS land—
Losing counties**

- < 15.6
- 15.6 to 31.2
- 31.2 to 46.8
- 46.8 to 62.4
- 62.4 to 78
- 78 to 93.6

Figure A11—Percentage of National Forest System land, counties losing eligibility, Revised 1993 versus 2004.

**Percent NFS land—
Gaining counties**

- < 15.6
- 15.6 to 31.2
- 31.2 to 46.8
- 46.8 to 62.4
- 62.4 to 78

Figure A12—Percentage of National Forest System land, counties gaining eligibility, Revised 1993 versus 2004.